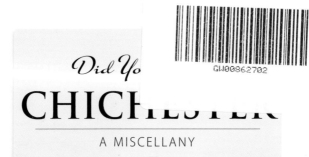

Did You
CHICHESTER
A MISCELLANY

Compiled by Julia Skinner
With particular reference to the work of Martin Andrew

THE FRANCIS FRITH COLLECTION

www.francisfrith.com

Based on a book first published in the United Kingdom in 2006 by The Francis Frith Collection®

This edition published exclusively for Oakridge in 2009 ISBN 978-1-84589-442-9

British Library Cataloguing in Publication Data

Did You Know? Chichester - A Miscellany
Compiled by Julia Skinner
With particular reference to the work of Martin Andrew

The Francis Frith Collection
Frith's Barn, Teffont,
Salisbury, Wiltshire SP3 5QP
Tel: +44 (0) 1722 716 376
Email: info@francisfrith.co.uk
www.francisfrith.com

Printed and bound in Singapore

Front Cover: **CHICHESTER, SOUTH STREET 1923** 73655p

CONTENTS

INTRODUCTION

The busy modern city of Chichester stands on historic foundations. During the period of Roman occupation of Britain, the coastal plain of Sussex was part of a 'grain factory' which produced corn for export to other parts of the Roman empire. The Roman palace at Fishbourne was an important administrative supply base for the early phases of the Roman conquest, and by the 2nd century AD the Roman town of Noviomagus, which lies under present-day Chichester, had developed as a centre of Roman culture and authority.

In medieval times wool was Chichester's major product, and there was a large export trade from its port. In later years first cloth and then corn also became important commodities. Chichester's medieval heritage is seen in its cathedral and other associated buildings, the Market Cross, and medieval churches in the city, although sadly all four of the medieval gatehouses into the walled city disappeared in the late 18th century. However, much of the external character of the houses both near the cathedral and in the city streets and lanes is Georgian. Despite some destruction and rebuilding in the second half of the 20th century, especially in the north-west quadrant and some stretches of North and East Street, there is still a pleasing cohesion to the city; a walk in the Pallants in the south-east quadrant, or around St Martin's Square in the north-east, is still satisfying for those who value a good Georgian townscape. The architecture demonstrates clearly that this period was one of wealth for Chichester, when the citizens, local gentry and merchants grew rich on shipping and the corn trade, cattle and milling. The city in its prosperous heyday acquired all the civilised and civic buildings necessary to corporate and city life: a Council House, Assembly Rooms, a Market House, and a Corn Exchange, the latter a massively confident Greek Doric temple-style building that is now a McDonald's restaurant.

Despite some bomb damage during the Second World War, modern redevelopment and considerable expansion, good things have also happened to Chichester in recent years, such as the Festival Theatre, pedestrianisation and traffic calming in the centre, and an increased awareness of the value of the city's splendid architecture and character. Chichester is bypassed by the A27, which was one of the earliest bypasses in the country. The overall impression left on the visitor is of a place on an intimate, humane scale, a feeling emphasised by its cathedral, which is one of the smallest in the country, not too showy and very much in keeping with the city. The story of Chichester is full of fascinating characters and events, of which this book can only provide a brief glimpse.

THE CATHEDRAL AND THE BISHOP'S PALACE 1892 29986

SUSSEX DIALECT WORDS AND PHRASES

'Windogs' - clouds blown across the sky by a strong wind.

'Knuckerhole' - a spring which rises in the South Downs.

'Squatelings' - female conversation or chatter.

'Twitten' - a narrow path between hedges.

'Loving mud' - sticky mud.

'Outlandish' - foreign, out of the local neighbourhood.

'Looker' - a shepherd.

'Slummocky' - messy, untidy.

'Swimey' - feeling sick or faint.

'You may push and you may shov
But I'm hemmed if I'll be druv
... For Sussex will be Sussex, and Sussex won't be druv.'

HAUNTED CHICHESTER

A local tradition says the Bishop of Chichester is warned about his impending death when a heron perches on the cathedral's spire.

The grounds of Graylingwell Hospital, now the headquarters of the Sussex Weald and Downs National Health Service Trust, are said to be haunted by the ghost of a monk.

The Kingley Vale, a few miles north of Chichester, is said to be haunted by ghosts associated with the burial mounds in the area; in the past these were believed to have connections with a 9th-century battle between Saxons and Danish (Viking) raiders that took place nearby. There was also an old belief that the trees in the area could move about at night.

The ghost of a Roman soldier is supposed to walk the boundary of the ancient city walls of Chichester at night. He also pops into the Chichester Inn from time to time, although only the top portion of his body is visible; his appearance is always accompanied by a noticeable drop in temperature.

Goodwood House, near Chichester, is linked with stories about a phantom coach and horses.

CHICHESTER MISCELLANY

Chichester's cathedral, and especially its 277ft-high tower, dominates the city and the countryside for miles around, as indeed it should, for it is the mother church of Sussex. The cathedral was started in the late 11th century by Bishop Ralph Luffa, and in the main is still a Norman building, with later additions. It suffered a disastrous fire in 1187 which led to the building of a new east end and much refacing, as well as stone vaults being added throughout. Two towers were blown down in 1210, and the rebuilt central tower received a soaring 271ft-high spire in 1300. The tower and spire collapsed in 1861, and the spire was rebuilt under the supervision of Sir George Gilbert Scott, who added another six feet to its height. The magnificent cathedral building includes a shrine to St Richard, Romanesque stone carvings, a dazzling modern altar tapestry by John Piper, windows by Marc Chagall and a painting by Graham Sutherland.

The street plan of the walled city of Chichester is based on its Roman predecessor, Noviomagus, which was divided into quarters by North, South, East and West Streets, laid out on the normal Roman plan of north-south and east-west roads intersecting at the centre of the town. These roads still survive almost on their original alignment, but the minor roads within the city do not; this seems to indicate that in later times the city shrank within its walls, with settlement only along its axial roads. The south-west section of the city is dominated by the Norman cathedral. Above ground, however, little of either the Roman town or the later medieval city remains, as Chichester was almost entirely rebuilt at the end of the 18th century.

Chichester started life as a Roman town, founded in the first century AD in the earliest years of Roman Britain. The Roman town was called Noviomagus Regnensium, which means 'the new market place of the Regnenses tribe'.

Around AD200, the Roman town of Noviomagus acquired stone defensive walls to replace the earlier fortifications of an earth bank and ditch. Although they are much added to, and were refaced and rebuilt during medieval times, the walls survive. They were adapted in the 18th century into rampart walks along much of the northern half of the city. Good views of the south-west section can be seen across playing fields; it is only in the south-east quarter, or 'Quadrant' as these sections are known locally, that much of the wall has disappeared or is hidden.

In 1960, nearly nineteen centuries after it was built, the Roman palace of Fishbourne was discovered, one of the largest and most opulent buildings north of the Alps. Believed to have been built in the early years of the Roman occupation, in about AD75, it was a palace fit for a king, with elaborately planned rooms, an extensive underfloor hypocaust system (hot air central heating), stone buildings around a courtyard and a second court with gardens running down to the sea. The first major evidence exposed was a mosaic floor; many more mosaics of the highest artistic quality, together with extensive building foundations, are now contained in special buildings erected to protect them, while part of the courtyard gardens have been restored. The mosaic floor shown in photograph F132002, below, has a centrepiece of Cupid riding a dolphin.

FISHBOURNE, THE ROMAN PALACE c1968 F132002

THE BELL TOWER 1892 30001

Did You Know?
CHICHESTER
A MISCELLANY

The cathedral's detached bell tower, shown in photograph 00001, opposite, was built to carry the bells because the cathedral's central tower had become too weak to allow the bells to be rung. Suitably massive, the bell tower was started about 1375, but was not completed until about 1440; in 1873 it suffered the indignity of being proposed for conversion to a municipal water tower. Chichester Cathedral is the only medieval cathedral in Europe to have a separate bell tower.

In AD477 the Saxon warlord Aelle and his sons Cissa, Cymen and Wlencing arrived at the south coast in three ships. Landing near West Wittering, they seized Noviomagus and established the kingdom of the South Saxons, known nowadays as Sussex. The old Roman town was given to Cissa and it became known as 'Cissas ceastre', or 'Cissa's camp', which later became the modern 'Chichester'.

In 1829, two 12th-century panels of Purbeck stone, with scenes depicting the biblical story of the raising of Lazarus from the dead, were found built into the eastern piers of the crossing of the cathedral. They have now been re-erected in the south aisle of the choir, and are considered by many to be among the greatest works of Romanesque monumental sculpture in England. The deeply-drilled eyes of the figures would originally have been inlaid with metal or precious stones.

During the First World War, the first Kitchener battalion of the Royal Sussex Regiment was recruited in Chichester. 323 local men from this battalion were killed on the Western Front.

ST MARY'S ALMSHOUSES 1898 42682

The St Mary's Almshouses building is one of the most remarkable survivals in Europe: a virtually unchanged medieval hospital, its hall and chapel dating from the late 13th century (see photograph 42682 above). Originally, the hospital and the chapel, divided by a beautifully carved screen, were housed in the same building so that the sick could still benefit from religious services. The sick-bay hall was divided into almshouses in the 17th century, which preserved the buildings intact.

In 1588 the people of Chichester provided a small ship called 'The John' for the fleet to fight the Spanish Armada.

The opening of the branch canal to the Portsmouth-Arun Canal in 1823 benefited the city's trade, and also allowed more goods to reach Chichester via the canal basin with its warehouses. Later in the 19th century, boats and barges laden with coking coal fed the city's gas works, strategically placed by the canal basin. Ironically, the Chichester Branch canal survives, together with the stretch of the Portsmouth-Arun between Hunstan, where the branch joined it, and the outlet into Chichester Harbour: the rest of the canal is now earthworks, long since dried-up. Photograph 42684, below, was taken from the towpath beside Poyntz Bridge, a still-surviving swing bridge dated 1820, looking towards the city's canal basin and the gas works.

FROM THE CANAL 1898 42684

Chichester's splendid Market Cross is sited at the intersection of four main roads that date from the Roman period. The eight-sided Caen stone building was built in 1501 by Bishop Storey, on market land bought from the mayor and burgesses for £10, after encroachment of merchants' shops on to the market place had displaced the poor from the market area. The bishop's Market Cross was specifically planned so that 'the poore people shall here after stand or sell eny Chafer (goods) Within the said crosse' in a sheltered space free of market tolls. Octagonal in plan, the Cross has an ogeed arch to each facet, four facing down the principal streets. Elaborate flying buttresses rise from pinnacles to support a Georgian cupola, which replaced a stone structure with saints in niches. The clock, the ball and the iron weathervane were all added in 1746. The original much-worn stone bench around the central column is still a popular place to sit today.

During the Civil War, the people of Chichester associated with the Church tended to support Charles I, whilst the merchants were for Parliament. When the king raised his standard in 1642 the High Sheriff, Sir Edward Ford, rode into Chichester to claim it for the king, and imprisoned those he suspected of being Parliamentary sympathisers. A Parliamentarian force under Sir William Waller soon arrived, and after a siege lasting several days the Royalist forces surrendered. One of Chichester's most prominent Parliamentarian supporters, and its Member of Parliament, William Cawley, managed to escape during the siege; he was later one of the signatories on the death warrant of Charles I. He was forced to flee the country after the restoration of Charles II, but his name lives on in Chichester in the Cawley almshouses in Broyle Road, which he endowed.

SOUTH STREET 1923 73655

Much that can be seen on the right of photograph 73655 of
South Street, above, has now gone, including the splendid
and rather alarming optician's spectacles sign and Lang's
Tea Rooms beyond, which also advertises 'Good Beds'. On
the left, most is still intact, although the line of shop blinds,
so characteristic of late 19th- and early 20th-century street
scenes, has now gone; in some places, bylaws stated that shop
blinds had to be high enough for a policeman wearing his
helmet to be able to walk underneath.

Under the floor of the nave of Chichester Cathedral is a Roman
mosaic floor which dates from the second century; it can be viewed
through a glass window.

After the Norman Conquest of 1066 Sussex was divided into six administrative areas called 'rapes', one of which was the Rape of Chichester. This was given to Roger de Montgomery, Earl of Arundel, one of William the Conqueror's most powerful lords. In 1086 the king commissioned a great survey of his newly won territories, which became known as the Domesday Book. This survey recorded Chichester's population as being 1,300, with about 160 dwellings.

Photograph 22617, below, shows the superb bronze bust of Charles I in a niche in the Market Cross which was installed in 1669, soon after his son, Charles II, was restored to the throne, as a judicious mark of Chichester's loyalty.

THE MARKET CROSS 1890 22617

Horseracing on the Downs at Goodwood was started in 1802
by the Duke of Richmond and Gordon, and the horseshoe-
shaped course remains largely unchanged. This beautiful
course with its spectacular views across the Downs to the sea,

nicknamed 'Glorious Goodwood', soon became established, and since 1814 the five-day meeting every July has been a key event in the English social calendar.

GOODWOOD, THE RACECOURSE 1904 52291

THE WAR MEMORIAL
1923 73664

In July 1921 Chichester's fine war memorial was unveiled in Eastgate Square, just beyond the city walls. Photograph 73664, opposite, shows the memorial in its original position; it was later moved to Litten Gardens to avoid inconveniencing motor traffic. In the background of the photograph is the Unicorn, which was demolished in the 1950s to make way for the premises of the Chichester Observer.

Chichester's MP William Cawley was forced to live abroad for the rest of his life after the restoration of Charles II in 1660, as he had been one of the men who signed Charles I's death warrant. During his exile he often expressed the wish to be buried after his death in the chapel of the almshouses in Broyle Road in Chichester which he had endowed; however, it was felt that it would be unlikely that the body of a regicide would be allowed back into the country, and he was buried in the Swiss town of Vernay, after his death in 1680. In 1816, during repairs to the floor of the chapel of the Cawley almshouses, workmen discovered a vault containing two coffins and a body wrapped in lead, and it is believed that this is almost certainly that of Cawley, whose body was at some time secretly brought back to Chichester and buried where he had wished. A small plaque in the chapel now marks where his remains have been re-interred.

To the north of Greyfriars in Priory Park is a mound, now municipalised, which is all that remains of Chichester's castle. This was a motte (an artificial hill) surrounded by a ditch and rampart with a bailey (a wooden palisade); there is no evidence that the castle was later built in stone. The castle was briefly taken and occupied by French soldiers in 1216, and was won back in 1217, after which it was demolished.

Near the bowling green in Priory Park is an 18th-century statue of Moses striking a rock to bring forth water, which once stood on the conduit house at the public drinking supply fountain in South Street. Later the statue was kept in the cathedral vault of the surgeon William Guy, whose grandson presented it to Priory Park in 1873 in his memory (see C84085, opposite).

We know from an inscription found in 1723 (now on display at the Assembly Rooms in North Street) that there was a temple dedicated to Neptune and Minerva in the Roman town of Noviomagus Regnensium. The inscription records that the temple was erected by permission of Tiberius Claudius Cogidubnus (or Togidubnus), the 'great king in Britain'.

The 'Anglo-Saxon Chronicle' records that a battle was fought between men from Chichester and Viking raiders in AD895: 'they went up plundering in Sussex nigh Chichester; but the townsmen put them to flight, and slew many hundreds of them, and took some of their ships'.

One of the most important industries of medieval Chichester was needlemaking. Names recorded of people living in the town in the 13th century (le Nedeler and le Aguiller), show that the industry was established at an early date, but it suffered after the siege of the Civil War in 1642, when the needleworkers' area around St Pancras was destroyed. The last recorded needlemaker in Chichester was Mr Scale, the parish clerk, who was working in 1783. The industry is remembered in the name of the road between St Pancras and the Hornet, The Needlemakers.

THE ROYAL WEST SUSSEX HOSPITAL c1965 C84139

Photograph C84139, above, shows the Royal West Sussex Hospital, which has now been closed. Its main block, a long stuccoed range of 1828 (though largely reconstructed in 1913), with its central pediment seen here between the trees, is now converted to flats as part of King George Gardens, an estate of neo-Georgian houses which occupy the site of the other hospital buildings.

The cathedral occupies much of the south-west quadrant of the city and gives it a distinctively medieval character, entered by a medieval gateway from South Street. As well as the cathedral itself, many of the nearby houses and buildings contain medieval work, including the Vicar's Close, the Bishop's Palace and the Chantry.

Where the Portsmouth-Arun Canal, opened in 1813, reached the estuaries east of Portsmouth, a lock was formed and a canal basin built. This is the basis of the Chichester Marina, which grew up immediately north of Salterns Lock to serve the leisure sailing and boating for which this area is now famous. How many owners of the increasingly luxurious boats berthed there realise that the basin started life as the terminus for a canal whose promoters in their 1817 prospectus gave one of their principal aims as 'the improvement and better cultivation of the circumjacent country by the conveyance of manure'?

THE YACHT BASIN c1965 C84173

Built in flint in 1790-1800 for Charles Lennox, 3rd Duke of
Richmond and Gordon, Goodwood House near Chichester was
designed by James Wyatt and includes in its structure parts of

GOODWOOD HOUSE c1965 G33107

26

a previous house built in 1720. It has spectacular views of the South Downs and Chichester Cathedral, and contains paintings by Canaletto, Van Dyck and Stubbs.

BOSHAM, THE CHURCH AND THE GREEN 1903 50919

The village of Bosham is at the end of an arm from Chichester harbour. The straight and wide road leading to the quay creates the impression that this present-day fishing village and yachting centre was once a place of much greater importance, as indeed it was. The Romans, the Saxons and the Vikings (who stole the church bells) used the area for invasion, and King Canute had a palace here. Bosham is traditionally the place where the king tried to hold back the tide, in an effort to prove to his fawning courtiers that he was not all-powerful, as they suggested. In photograph 50919, above, we look past the fishermen, nowadays replaced by leisure yachtsmen, to the Anglo-Saxon church, which is believed to be the burial place of King Canute's second daughter, who died in infancy.

Soon after 1269 the Grey Friars (Franciscans) began to build a sumptuous church in the north-east quadrant of Chichester on land donated by Richard, Earl of Cornwall. However, they got no further than building the choir, and the great arch seen in photograph C84036, below, intended to lead into the nave, was blocked up by 1300. Dissolved by Henry VIII in 1538, the church had many subsequent uses, including service as the city's guildhall and as an archaeological store. This fine building is situated in what is now a park which was given by the Duke of Richmond and Gordon to the city in 1918 as a war memorial and for the people of Chichester to enjoy.

GREYFRIARS, PRIORY PARK c1955 C84036

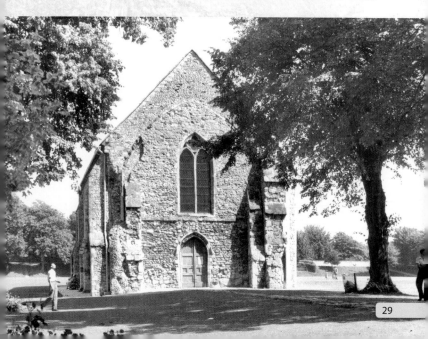

The view shown in photograph 22621, opposite, taken from the rampart walls, is a nostalgic one, as all the buildings but the cathedral have now disappeared. Modern flats and houses have replaced those on the left, and County Council buildings those on the right.

Rolls-Royce Motor Cars, part of the BMW Group, invested £65 million in its new manufacturing plant and head office at Goodwood, which opened in January 2003 with the creation of 550 new jobs. The new plant was opened with a fanfare with the launch of the Rolls-Royce Phantom, which has rapidly become the best selling super-luxury car in the world. Around 90% of the Phantoms built at Goodwood are exported around the world. A second model built at Goodwood, the Phantom with Extended Wheelbase, was launched in December 2005, and will be joined by a third model - a new convertible - in 2007.

Chichester Harbour is the only area of outstanding natural beauty in the country that includes a harbour, and is visited by around 1.5 million people every year. Many of the visitors come to watch the 50,000 birds that live in or visit Chichester Harbour each year, and it is believed to be the most important site on the south coast of England for waterfowl. There is also a small colony of harbour seals living in the area.

One of the tombs in Chichester Cathedral is that of the Earl of Arundel and his wife, whose effigies are represented hand in hand. This tomb inspired Philip Larkin to write his famous poem 'An Arundel Tomb', which begins *'Side by side, their faces blurred, The earl and countess lie in stone'* and ends with the famous line *'What will survive of us is love'.*

TOWER CROSS 1890 22621

Did You Know?
CHICHESTER
A MISCELLANY

GRAYLINGWELL HOSPITAL 1898 42678

Photograph 42678, above, shows Graylingwell Hospital, which in Victorian times was known as the county lunatic asylum. It is now the headquarters of the Sussex Weald and Downs National Health Service Trust. Note the tall water tower in the photograph, which, like the cathedral spire, can be seen for miles around.

Chichester was in the front line during the Second World War, and was surrounded by airfields at Tangmere, Westhampnett, Funtington, Selsey, Apuldram and Thorney Island. The city experienced three air raids, in 1941, 1943 and 1944, the worst of which was in 1943, when fifteen people were killed. Towards the end of the war, Bishop Otter College was used as an RAF control unit for 56 squadrons supporting the Normandy landings in 1944.

32

Many of the sections of the Mulberry Harbour used for the Normandy landings in 1944 were assembled at various points around Chichester Harbour, and were launched there before being towed to the assembly point off the Isle of Wight. Remains of some of the launch sites can still be seen - their concrete slipways look like giant squares of chocolate.

Despite having a three-sided cloister, Chichester's cathedral was not a monastic foundation, so the cloisters serve to enclose a tranquil grassy area known as The Paradise. St Richard, whose brightly painted statue is in the niche above the double arch seen in photograph 29995 (below), was Bishop of Chichester from 1245 to 1253, and was canonised by the Pope in 1262. There is also a modern statue of St Richard by Philip Jackson outside the cathedral in the main concourse.

THE CATHEDRAL, THE CLOISTERS AND ST RICHARD'S PORCH 1892 29995

When Ascot commemorated the accession of Edward VII in
1901 by building a new grandstand, the Duke of Richmond
responded by building an imposing two-tier grandstand
at Goodwood to accommodate 10,000 people, at a cost of

GOODWOOD, THE RACECOURSE 1904 52290

£40,000. Edward VII was a frequent visitor to the racecourse; he was often seen in the Royal Box at the western end of the new grandstand, which was built by 1904 (see 52296, page 36).

GOODWOOD, ILLUSTRATION OF THE GRANDSTAND, THE ROYAL BOX 1904
52296

Chichester's Sloe Fair was originally held in Oaklands Park, on what is now the area of a car park near the Festival Theatre. Permission to hold a fair was granted by Henry II in 1107, making it one of the oldest fairs in the country. At one time the fair lasted for five days, but is now held on 20 October each year. It was named the Sloe Fair after the sloe trees in the area, which are in fruit at this time of the year.

One of Chichester's finest houses is Pallant House at North Pallant, now the Pallant House Gallery, which holds one of the best collections of 20th-century British art in the country. It was built for Henry Peckham, who was a Chichester wine merchant, in 1712, and has also been known as Dodo House because of the strange birds carved on the gate pillars. The story goes that Henry Peckham wanted ostriches on the pillars because these birds appear on his family coat of arms, but the person who carved them had never seen an ostrich, and the final result was birds that looked more like the now-extinct dodo.

In the District Museum is a reminder of crime and punishment in Chichester medieval-style: in the museum is the mobile whipping post-cum-stocks which used to be wheeled around the city whilst onlookers threw refuse and abuse at the offender who was locked in them. Humiliation was felt to be an integral factor in punishment in those days, and gave local people the chance to show their displeasure.

Chichester's world-renowned Festival Theatre is a thoroughly modern building designed by Powell and Moya. The 1,206 seat Festival Theatre was the first in this country to have an open 'thrust' stage which the audience sits around on three sides, allowing a much closer involvement with the actors than with a traditional proscenium arch stage. The Festival Theatre was the brainchild of a former mayor, Leslie Evershed-Martin, and opened in 1962. Its first director was none other than Sir Laurence Olivier. The highlight of the theatre's programme is the Summer Festival which runs from April to September and features a wide range of plays from classics to contemporary writing.

THE FESTIVAL THEATRE c1965 C84118

Three miles east of Chichester is the old RAF Tangmere airfield, which played an important role in the Second World War during the Battle of Britain. As well as being a front line fighter plane base during the war, Tangmere was also where SOE agents would leave for secret operations in occupied France aboard 'Black Lysander' flights. The airfield is now home to the Tangmere Military Aviation Museum, and amongst the exhibits is some of the equipment used by these special agents. The airfield also holds an important place in aviation history as it was home to the world speed record-breaking aircraft of the High Speed Flight in the post-war years - Neville Duke's world-record-breaking Hawker Hunter plane can also be seen here.

Census records show that in 1801 Chichester's total population was 30,643; in 1901 it had risen to 52,493, and by 2001 the population was 106,445. By contrast, better healthcare, nutrition and lifestyles mean that the rate of infant mortality has declined over the same period: the census for 1851 found that 91 babies in every thousand in Chichester died in their first year; by 1911 the number had gone down to 69 in every thousand, and by the 2001 census the rate was 1 in every thousand.

The writer and traveller Daniel Defoe visited Chichester in the early 18th century, and was impressed with its cathedral, writing: 'From hence to … Chichester are 12 miles, and the most pleasant, beautiful country in England … The cathedral here is not the finest, but is far from being the most ordinary.' However, he was not so complimentary about the local society, saying 'I cannot say much of Chichester, in which, if six or seven good families were removed, there would not be much conversation, except what is to be found among the canons, and the dignitaries of the cathedral'. ('A Tour Through the Whole Island of Great Britain', 1724-27).

EAST STREET 1890 22622

THE MARKET CROSS FROM WEST STREET c1955 C84024

The following obituary was printed in the Chichester Observer in April 1915:

'The city has lost a remarkable personality with the death, on Saturday, of Mr John McKay, for many years church warden of St George's, Rumboldswhyke… He was born in Edinburgh on March 29th 1812 of pure Highland blood, being the only son of Wm. McKay of the parish of Reay, Caithness. His father, a soldier, died when he was very young, and before he was 13 Mr McKay also joined the Army. He served under George IV, through the reign of William IV, and the first part of the reign of Queen Victoria. Mr McKay was one of the troops who lined the route of Queen Victoria's coronation procession. He went to South Africa, where many years of his life were passed, and he took part in the earlier fighting with the Zulus and other native tribes. He was among the first body of British troops who crossed the Orange River. In Africa he had many adventures, which he remembered well, and could recall in a very interesting way. On one occasion he had been on a very long journey, and on his return to the settlement where he lived, found the place in the hands of the Zulus and all the inhabitants massacred. He acquired property in South Africa, and became closely acquainted with many of the leading Boer pioneers. Among them were the Bothas, and Mr McKay, who had a good education, was asked to act as tutor to the boy who afterwards became famous as General Louis Botha. He taught Louis Botha, and when the latter was over in England as part of the Boer deputation at the time of the war, he stayed in Chichester with his old tutor. Feeling ran high in the country at that time, and the visit, so natural in the circumstances, was the subject of much comment locally. Mr McKay spent the last 40 years of his life in Chichester, where he and his family were highly respected.'

CANON LANE ARCHWAY, SOUTH STREET 1890 22623

THE MARKET CROSS 1890 22618

An old rhyme about Sussex food, called 'Seven Good Things of
Sussex', mentions Chichester as being famous for the local lobster:

Of a score of good things found outside heaven
The land of Sussex was granted seven
The choicest of those I often feel
Is the oily, glutinous Pulborough eel
Though the Selsea cockle would be the best
The Chichester lobster's the lordliest dish
The herring of Rye is the tastiest dish
The mullet of Arundel would have my vote
If I could but forget the Amberley trout
The wheatear of Bourne whenever it's about.

(The wheatear is a small bird.)

NORTH STREET 1898 42677

SPORTING CHICHESTER

GOODWOOD MOTOR RACING.
Although competitive racing at the circuit ended in 1968, Goodwood still holds a special place in British motor racing history. Many of our top racers have connections with the course. Jackie Stewart was 'discovered' there during a test session, and went on to be World Formula One Champion. Two other World Champions, Mike Hawthorn and Graham Hill, had their first single-seat races at Goodwood. Another World Champion, Jim Clarke, competed at the course, as did the legendary Stirling Moss, probably the best driver never to win the world championship.

PRIORY PARK.
A small number of first-class cricket matches were played at Priory Park between 1852 and 1950. In the early days, notable games included Sussex against the All-England team, and Lord March's 11 against the Australians. The last first-class match at the park was when Sussex played Glamorgan in 1950.

JAMES LILLYWHITE.
Probably Chichester's most prominent cricketer was James Lillywhite. He was born in Westhampnett in 1842, a member of a prolific cricketing family, five of whom had played for Sussex. He toured Australia six times with England, although he played only two Test Matches. His most remarkable achievement though was the regularity of his appearances for his county. He played every match for Sussex from 1862 to 1881!

ALAN ARNELL.
Alan Arnell was probably the finest footballer produced by the city. 'The Cannonball Kid' was born in Chichester in 1933, and after being educated at and playing for the city's High School, Arnell played for Chichester City for two years. He was recruited by Portsmouth, and then moved to Liverpool, where he spent seven seasons, scoring 39 goals. He then made a successful move to Tranmere Rovers, where he scored a tremendous 41 goals in his first season.

QUIZ QUESTIONS

Answers on page 50.

1. In 1292 the Earl of Arundel was excommunicated by the Bishop of Chichester - a most serious punishment at that time - for what heinous crime?

2. Who was the Roman palace at Fishbourne built for?

3. How did a collapsed tower in Chichester fulfil an old prophecy?

4. Which historic item of sailing memorabilia is kept in Chichester's cathedral?

5. With which two European cities is Chichester twinned?

6. Which rock music supergroup has performed at Chichester Cathedral?

7. What is the name for inhabitants of Chichester?

8. What is the link between Chichester Harbour and James Bond, 007?

9. Chichester Cathedral was built c1070-75, but where was the religious centre in the area before this date?

10. Which church in the Chichester area features on the Bayeux Tapestry?

RECIPE

SLOE GIN

Ingredients

1kg/2lb sloes

175g/6oz sugar

1 bottle of gin (any cheap variety will do)

Chichester's Sloe Fair is held in October, and is named after the sloes (the fruit of the blackthorn tree) which are ripe in the hedgerows at this time of year. Sloe Gin can be made now, and will be ready to drink in time for Christmas. Traditionally it is best to wait until the first frosts have softened the skins of the fruits as this improves the flavour, but alternatively the gathered fruit can be put in a plastic bag and frozen for a few days.

   Gather about 1kg/2lb of sloes. Wash and dry them, and prick each sloe with a fork or skewer. Put the sloes with the sugar into a clean wide-topped jar - the jar should be about half filled. Top up the jar with gin, and close or seal the jar firmly. Store the Sloe Gin for 6-8 weeks (or up to 3 months if you can wait that long), giving the jar an occasional shake. When ready, strain the liquid, bottle and enjoy.

THE CATHEDRAL c1960 C84066

NORTH STREET c1955 C84070

RECIPES

These recipes for vegetables reflect Chichester's Roman heritage and are derived from a Roman cookery book, 'The Art of Cookery' by Apicius, which dates from the late 4th or early 5th century.

ARTICHOKES COOKED IN HERBS

Ingredients

6 young artichokes
A small sprig of rosemary
A small sprig of mint
A small sprig of lovage
A pinch of coriander seeds

A pinch of fennel seeds
Pepper
A drizzle of olive oil
A little water
A little white wine

Trim the artichoke tips and part of the stems, then place the artichokes in a pan, standing them on their trimmed tops with the stalks pointing up. Chop the herbs and add them to the pan with the remaining ingredients (except the oil) with enough water and wine to come halfway up the bulb of the artichokes. Bring to the boil and simmer gently, adding a little extra water if necessary, for 30-45 minutes until tender. Serve with the reduced cooking sauce, and a drizzle of olive oil poured over.

BRUSSELS SPROUTS WITH WALNUTS

Brussels sprouts are believed to have been cultivated in Italy in Roman times, although they did not became popular in northern Europe until the Middle Ages.

Ingredients

Brussels sprouts, Walnuts, Olive oil

Cook the brussels sprouts in a steamer. Heat the olive oil in a small pan. Break the walnuts into small pieces and cook them in the oil for a few minutes, then pour the oil and walnuts over the steamed brussels sprouts.

QUIZ ANSWERS

1. The Earl of Arundel was excommunicated by the Bishop of Chichester for walking his dog in the bishop's forest - presumably it was assumed that the earl was about to hunt the bishop's deer.

2. We shall probably never know for sure exactly who the Roman palace at Fishbourne was built for, but the most likely candidate is Tiberius Claudius Cogidubnus (or Togidubnus - opinion is divided on which is correct), King of the Regnenses, the local British tribe. He was a client king but appears to have been a firm ally of the Romans, and was given the title of King and Legate to the Roman Emperor in Britannia.

3. The spire and tower of Chichester's cathedral collapsed in 1861, fulfilling the prophecy in an old rhyme which said: 'If Chichester tower do fall, in England there's no King at all'. There was indeed no king at the time of the tower's collapse, for Queen Victoria was on the throne.

4. In the Sailors' Chapel of the cathedral is the pennant flown by Sir Francis Chichester on 'Gypsy Moth IV' when he became the first man to sail single-handedly around the world in 1966-67.

5. Chichester is twinned with Chartres in France and Ravenna in Italy.

6. Pink Floyd. The three remaining band members performed 'Fat Old Sun' and 'The Great Gig in the Sky' at Chichester Cathedral at the funeral of their manager, Steve O'Rourke, who died in October 2003. Reports in the media erroneously claimed that they played 'Wish You Were Here'.

7. Cicestrians.

8. In 1977, scenes from the James Bond film 'The Spy Who Loved Me' were filmed at Chichester Harbour.

9. The see of Chichester was founded to replace the diocese of the South Saxons which had been established by St Wilfrid at Selsey, a few miles away. After the Norman Conquest it was part of William I's policy to replace rural cathedrals with new sees in centres of urban population, and the bishopric was moved to Chichester in the 1070s. It was a fortunate decision in this case, as the church at Selsey eventually succumbed to coastal erosion and now lies beneath the sea off Selsey Bill.

10. The church at Bosham features on the Bayeux Tapestry, for in 1064 King Edward the Confessor's brother-in-law Harold Godwinson (later King Harold) sailed from Bosham to Normandy, and set in train the events that led to the Battle of Hastings and his own death. It is not clear whether Harold's visit was accident or design - some accounts say that Edward had sent Harold to see William, but others say that Harold only ended up in Normandy after being shipwrecked. As shown on the Bayeux Tapestry, Harold agreed (or was forced) to swear on holy relics that after King Edward's death he would uphold William's claim to the English throne. When Harold broke his vow, William made this one of his justifications for invading England. Because a sacred vow appeared to have been broken, William was also able to call upon the support of the Pope for the Norman Conquest.

FRANCIS FRITH

PIONEER VICTORIAN PHOTOGRAPHER

Francis Frith, founder of the world-famous photographic archive, was a complex and multi-talented man. A devout Quaker and a highly successful Victorian businessman, he was philosophical by nature and pioneering in outlook. By 1855 he had already established a wholesale grocery business in Liverpool, and sold it for the astonishing sum of £200,000, which is the equivalent today of over £15,000,000. Now in his thirties, and captivated by the new science of photography, Frith set out on a series of pioneering journeys up the Nile and to the Near East.

INTRIGUE AND EXPLORATION

He was the first photographer to venture beyond the sixth cataract of the Nile. Africa was still the mysterious 'Dark Continent', and Stanley and Livingstone's historic meeting was a decade into the future. The conditions for picture taking confound belief. He laboured for hours in his wicker dark-room in the sweltering heat of the desert, while the volatile chemicals fizzed dangerously in their trays. Back in London he exhibited his photographs and was 'rapturously cheered' by members of the Royal Society. His reputation as a photographer was made overnight.

VENTURE OF A LIFE-TIME

By the 1870s the railways had threaded their way across the country, and Bank Holidays and half-day Saturdays had been made obligatory by Act of Parliament. All of a sudden the working man and his family were able to enjoy days out, take holidays, and see a little more of the world.

With typical business acumen, Francis Frith foresaw that these new tourists would enjoy having souvenirs to commemorate their days out. For the next thirty years he travelled the country by train and by pony and trap, producing fine photographs of seaside resorts and beauty spots that were keenly bought by millions of Victorians. These prints were painstakingly pasted into family albums and pored over during the dark nights of winter, rekindling precious memories of summer excursions. Frith's studio was soon supplying retail shops all over the country, and by 1890 F Frith & Co had become the greatest specialist photographic publishing company in the world, with over 2,000 sales outlets, and pioneered the picture postcard.

FRANCIS FRITH'S LEGACY

Francis Frith had died in 1898 at his villa in Cannes, his great project still growing. By 1970 the archive he created contained over a third of a million pictures showing 7,000 British towns and villages.

Frith's legacy to us today is of immense significance and value, for the magnificent archive of evocative photographs he created provides a unique record of change in the cities, towns and villages throughout Britain over a century and more. Frith and his fellow studio photographers revisited locations many times down the years to update their views, compiling for us an enthralling and colourful pageant of British life and character.

We are fortunate that Frith was dedicated to recording the minutiae of everyday life. For it is this sheer wealth of visual data, the painstaking chronicle of changes in dress, transport, street layouts, buildings, housing and landscape that captivates us so much today, offering us a powerful link with the past and with the lives of our ancestors.

Computers have now made it possible for Frith's many thousands of images to be accessed almost instantly. The archive offers every one of us an opportunity to examine the places where we and our families have lived and worked down the years. Its images, depicting our shared past, are now bringing pleasure and enlightenment to millions around the world a century and more after his death.

For further information visit: www.francisfrith.com

INTERIOR DECORATION

Frith's photographs can be seen framed and as giant wall murals in thousands of pubs, restaurants, hotels, banks, retail stores and other public buildings throughout Britain. These provide interesting and attractive décor, generating strong local interest and acting as a powerful reminder of gentler days in our increasingly busy and frenetic world.

FRITH PRODUCTS

All Frith photographs are available as prints and posters in a variety of different sizes and styles. In the UK we also offer a range of other gift and stationery products illustrated with Frith photographs, although many of these are not available for delivery outside the UK – see our web site for more information on the products available for delivery in your country.

THE INTERNET

Over 100,000 photographs of Britain can be viewed and purchased on the Frith web site. The web site also includes memories and reminiscences contributed by our customers, who have personal knowledge of localities and of the people and properties depicted in Frith photographs. If you wish to learn more about a specific town or village you may find these reminiscences fascinating to browse. Why not add your own comments if you think they would be of interest to others? See **www.francisfrith.com**

PLEASE HELP US BRING FRITH'S PHOTOGRAPHS TO LIFE

Our authors do their best to recount the history of the places they write about. They give insights into how particular towns and villages developed, they describe the architecture of streets and buildings, and they discuss the lives of famous people who lived there. But however knowledgeable our authors are, the story they tell is necessarily incomplete.

Frith's photographs are so much more than plain historical documents. They are living proofs of the flow of human life down the generations. They show real people at real moments in history; and each of those people is the son or daughter of someone, the brother or sister, aunt or uncle, grandfather or grandmother of someone else. All of them lived, worked and played in the streets depicted in Frith's photographs.

We would be grateful if you would give us your insights into the places shown in our photographs: the streets and buildings, the shops, businesses and industries. Post your memories of life in those streets on the Frith website: what it was like growing up there, who ran the local shop and what shopping was like years ago; if your workplace is shown tell us about your working day and what the building is used for now. Read other visitors' memories and reconnect with your shared local history and heritage. With your help more and more Frith photographs can be brought to life, and vital memories preserved for posterity, and for the benefit of historians in the future.

Wherever possible, we will try to include some of your comments in future editions of our books. Moreover, if you spot errors in dates, titles or other facts, please let us know, because our archive records are not always completely accurate—they rely on 140 years of human endeavour and hand-compiled records. You can email us using the contact form on the website.

Thank you!

For further information, trade, or author enquiries
please contact us at the address below:

**The Francis Frith Collection, Frith's Barn, Teffont,
Salisbury, Wiltshire, England SP3 5QP.**

Tel: +44 (0)1722 716 376 Fax: +44 (0)1722 716 881
e-mail: sales@francisfrith.co.uk **www.francisfrith.com**